In Kazakhstan, the children's TV show the Teletubbies was banned by personal order of the president on the grounds that Tinky Winky "was a sexual pervert."

◆◆◆

In 2013, a pig in Australia stole 18 beers from a campsite, got drunk, and then tried to fight a cow.

◆◆◆

Infinite Monkey Theorem states that monkeys with typewriters and infinite amount of time could produce the entire works of Shakespeare. This theorem was tried out in real life, but only for a month. The six monkeys wrote five pages of S, slammed the keyboard with a stone and took a sh*t on it.

◆◆◆

In older versions of Little Red Riding Hood, the girl and the wolf eat grandma together.

Albert Einstein had a silk bathrobe that he would "accidentally" let open in front of certain women. He would then make a move based on their reaction.

NASA had to re-label the p*nis sleeve for urinating in space suits from "small, medium, and large" to "large, gigantic, and humungous" because astronauts would only choose the large and they kept slipping off.

There's an annual lying competition in England, where competitors from around the world have five minutes to tell the biggest and most convincing lie they can. Politicians and lawyers are banned from entering because they're thought to be too good at it.

During the Cold War, USA considered airdropping enormous condoms labeled "Medium" into USSR, to demoralize them against an anatomically superior American Army.

In 2012, a court in Italy ruled that telling a man he has "no balls" is a crime, punishable with a fine.

A man in Shaanxi, China, recently realized that the long-handled, blunt-ended object he'd been using for 25 years to crack walnuts was actually a live hand grenade.

When monkeys are taught how to use money, they start to rob other monkeys and use the money to pay for sex.

St. Lawrence was roasted alive on a giant grill during the persecution. He joked with his tormentors, "Turn me over – I am done on this side". He is now the patron saint of cooks, comedians, and firefighters.

The bell rung to mark the death of Ivan the Terrible's son Dmitri was tried for treason, found guilty and exiled to Siberia.

A Chinese man sued his wife for being too ugly and the Court agreed awarding him US$115,000.

There was a TV show in Germany where 12 contestants donated their sperm and viewers watched to see whose sperm reached the egg first. The winner won a Porsche.

Iran arrested 14 squirrels for spying in 2007.

Men process the voices of other males with the same part of the brain that processes simple sounds like car engines and machinery, but they handle female voices with the part of the brain that processes music.

A guinea pig named Randy broke into a female enclosure and impregnated over 100 female guinea pigs.

The U.S. government's "official expert" on Marijuana from 1938 to 1962 once testified in court, under oath, that he had smoked marijuana and it turned him into a bat.

New Yorkers bite 10 times more people than sharks do worldwide.

In 2011, when a Russian man named Viktor Jasinski tried to rob a hair salon, he ended up as the victim when the female shop owner Olga Zajac overpowered him, tied him up naked and then used him as a sex slave for three days.

The CIA spent $20 million USD in the 60's training cats to spy on the Soviets – The first spy cat was hit by a taxi.

Over the course of two weeks, a single human male produces enough sperm to impregnate every fertile woman on the planet.

In Japan 'Jersey Shore' is known as 'Macaroni Rascals'.

Boris Yeltsin, when he was president of Russia, was found by White House secret service drunk and in his underwear on Pennsylvania Ave, trying to call a cab to get some pizza.

There is a "white man" café in Tokyo, where Japanese ladies ring a bell to summon tuxedo-wearing caucasians who respond with "yes, princess?" and serve them cake.

There is a Pirate Stock Exchange in Somalia, where anyone can invest with money or weapons, and bet on the result of the hijacking.

In 1978 a man with a shotgun held a Melbourne cafe hostage until his mother turned up in her night gown and hit him over the head with her handbag. He gave himself up soon after.

When doctors go on strike, the death rate stays level or drops.

MI6 once hacked an Al-Qaeda website and replaced instructions on how to make a bomb with a cupcake recipe.

Pineapples contain an enzyme that breaks down proteins in your mouth. So when you eat a pineapple, it is eating you back.

Every week in Japan, there's a widely popular, five minute long TV program that features a girl running up a hill. That's the entire show and each week, there's a different girl and a different hill. The show is called "Zenryoku Saka".

Ryan Gosling got his role in The Notebook because the director thought he was neither handsome nor cool.

In 2014, the city of Bogota, Colombia employed 420 mimes to poke fun at pedestrians and drivers who didn't follow the rules. As a result, traffic fatalities dropped by more than half, from an average of around 1300 to about 600.

Research shows that, for luxury brands, the ruder the sales staff, the higher the sales.

Russian voters used to have a box on their ballots to vote for "against all".

In Stockholm, there is a speed camera lottery where good drivers can win money from the fines of speeding drivers.

In the 1970s Intervision Song Contest, the Communist equivalent to Eurovision, viewers would vote by turning on lights at a given moment; power plants would measure the load to help determine the winner.

There is a site that offers a fake internet girlfriend service for $250 a month. This includes setting up a profile on a social networking site like Facebook to publicly communicate with you, making up to 2 public phone calls and getting about 10 text messages.

The Scottish town of Dull has formed a "Trinity of Tedium" with the towns of Boring (U.S.) and Bland (Australia).

Fiji Water once ran a campaign stating "The label says Fiji because it's not bottled in Cleveland". The city of Cleveland responded by testing both Fiji water and their own tap water. They found 6.4 micrograms of arsenic in Fiji water, and none in their own.

Radioactive wild boars are wreaking havoc in towns nearby the Fukushima nuclear power plant, causing an estimated $15 million in damage.

"Surprise me" were the last words of the 100 year-old, legendary comedian Bob Hope, responding to his wife's questions regarding where he would like to be buried.

Stalin had a secret lab to analyze the feces of other foreign leaders for the purpose of constructing psychological profiles. For example, a leader with high levels of tryptophan was assumed to be calm and approachable, while a lack of potassium indicated a nervous disposition.

A guy in Arizona wrote his address on $1 bills pleading that they be sent back to him and he gets them back from all over the world, up to $94/month.

Ravens get stoned by rubbing chewed-up ants on their feathers.

Between 1960 and 1977, the secret number authorising US presidents, to launch nuclear missiles was 00000000.

Refined sugar is more addictive than cocaine.

In 2010, a would-be suicide bomber in Russia was killed after a spam text message set off his explosives.

In 2009, Nigerian Police arrested a goat on suspicion of attempted armed robbery.

In 2014, an American exchange student in Germany had to be rescued by firefighters after getting stuck in a vagina sculpture.

In 2015, two day care employees in New Jersey were imprisoned for running a toddler "fight club" among a dozen boys and girls aged 4-6.

While sudden heart attacks during sex are rare, 75% of them happen to men who are cheating on their wives.

The average high school kid today has the same level of anxiety as the average psychiatric patient in the early 1950's.

The dinosaur noises in the "Jurassic Park" movie were made from recordings of tortoise sex.

In 2010, the Mongolian Navy consisted of a single tugboat manned by seven men and only one of them knew how to swim.

Every human being starts out as an asshole: it's the first part of the body to form in the womb.

Saddam Hussein used Whitney Houston's song "I will always love you" for his 2002 campaign.

YouTube star Grumpy Cat earned more money than Oscar-Winning Actress Gwyneth Paltrow in 2014.

Greek philosopher Chrysippus is said to have died of laughter after getting his donkey drunk, trying to eat figs.

Everyone thought Abraham Lincoln was ugly, including himself. Once when he was accused of being "two-faced," he replied, "If I had two faces, would I be wearing this one?".

Alexander the Great, Napoleon, Mussolini and Hitler, all suffered from ailurophobia, the fear of cats.

Isaac Newton was a Member of Parliament for a year and said only one sentence: he asked a nearby usher to close an open window.

A fortune cookie company once got the lottery numbers right, resulting in 110 winners and an investigation.

◆◆◆

There is a bill known as the "Cheeseburger Bill" which makes it illegal for people to sue food companies for making them obese.

The Spanish for 'when pigs fly' is 'when hens piss'.

If an ant gets drunk, his fellow comrade will carry him back to the nest to sleep off the alcohol.

Bottlenose dolphins like to do drugs by finding pufferfish, (which produce a powerful neurotoxin and are deadly to eat) and gently chew on them to "get high" on a small amount of the toxin, and will even pass a pufferfish around to other dolphins to share the "drugs."

Australia's largest ever petition of 792,985 signatures was submitted to the parliament in 2000 to protest against rising beer prices.

Kellogg's was anti-sex and corn flakes were invented as part of an anti-masturbation crusade.

Benjamin Franklin and John Adams once shared a room and couldn't agree whether to open or shut the window. Franklin won by arguing until Adams fell asleep.

The British Navy uses Britney Spears' songs to scare off Somali pirates.

92% of public baby changing tables tested in the UK carried traces of cocaine.

In the 16th century, a London law forbade wife beating after 9:00 P.M., but only because the noise disturbed people's sleep.

Italian artist Piero Manzoni filled 90 tin cans with his feces, called it "Artist's sh*t" and sold them for up to €124,000 a tin.

The Japanese who survived the Titanic crash was called a coward in his country for not dying with the other passengers.

Japan's birth rate is so low that adult diapers are sold more than baby diapers.

The motto of Russia's nuclear strike missile force is: "After us, it is silence."

Netherlands voted "Swaffelen" as their word of the year in 2008. It means to repeatedly smack one's pen*s against someone or something.

It wasn't until the 1930's that production techniques improved to the point where toilet paper could be advertised as "splinter-free."

In 1998, Sony inadvertently released a camcorder that could see through clothes. When aimed at people wearing dark clothing, the night vision feature created an X-ray effect, meaning whatever was beneath became visible. Sony had to recall over 700,000 units after they discovered the issue.

One of the most popular marching songs for the Russian Military is the Spongebob Squarepants theme song.

ForgetMeNot is a superhero whose superpower is that everyone forgets about him. Even machines. He was also one of the original members of the X-Men it is just that they forget about him.

Bonobos, one of our most closely related primates, are rarely, if ever, found in zoos because they constantly have sex (both oral and genital) with each other regardless of their own age or sex.

At Andrew Jackson's funeral in 1845, his pet parrot had to be removed because it was swearing.

The brain has an "automatic p*nis maintenance function" to force erections if unused for too long.

In 2013, an American Airlines flight from Los Angeles to New York City made an unscheduled stop in Kansas City to offload a passenger, who wouldn't stop singing "I Will Always Love You."

Samuel L. Jackson had 'Bad Motherf*cker' engraved on the lightsaber that he used in Star Wars.

The Sami people of northern Finland use a measure called Poronkusema: the distance a reindeer can walk before needing to urinate.

Grunting in tennis is punishable by losing a point to the opponent. This is because some player's grunts, like Maria Sharapova's grunt is nearly equal to that of a lion's roar and this can affect how the opponent returns the ball.

One in five marriages in the world are between first cousins.

In 2010 a man from Arizona sold and "air guitar" on eBay for $5.5 and claimed it was used once at a Bon Jovi concert.

The average American woman now weighs as much as the average American man in the 1960s.

According to Cunningham's Law, "The best way to get the right answer on the Internet is not to ask a question, it is to post the wrong answer."

In Russia it's now Illegal to tell kids Gay People Exist.

There is a Norwegian nonprofit organization that makes porn to protect against tropical deforestation. Their name is F*ck For Forest.

The Russian mayor of Megion, west Siberia, banned excuses.

In North Korea, citizens are forced to choose one of 28 government-approved haircuts.

Beer was not considered an alcoholic beverage in Russia until 2013.

There is a Santa Claus University that teaches professional Santa Claus skills like toy knowledge, poses, and how to avoid lawsuits. A top-level Santa Claus can make up to $100,000 a year.

In exchange for Pepsi products, Russia gave Pepsi 17 submarines, a cruiser, a frigate, and a destroyer. At the time, it was 7th largest submarine fleet in the world.

The anti-piracy group responsible for the ad on all your DVDs was sued for stealing the theme song.

The first armoured presidential car was a Cadillac that had previously belonged to Al Capone.

A Mexican theme park stages a fake border crossing with a 7.5 mile night hike for about $18 a person.

Beauty pageants for children are banned in France. They are punishable with up to 2 years in prison and a €30,000 fine.

Norway's first aircraft hijacking was resolved after the hijacker surrendered his weapon in exchange for more beer.

In Soviet Russia, prisoners used to get tattoos of Lenin & Stalin, because guards were ordered not to shoot at images of national leaders.

Chinese students can get 7 years in jail for cheating on exams.

When The Office first aired in 2001, it had the second-lowest audience appreciation score on the BBC after women's bowling.

Godwin's Law: "As an online discussion grows longer, the probability of a comparison involving Hitler approaches 1"

US Air Force had a little known unit named Wild Weasel with the motto "You've gotta be sh*tting me", which was what some of the crews said when they were told their mission. It was a unit dedicated to hunting down anti-aircraft missile launchers using aircrafts.

McDonalds calls frequent buyers of their food "heavy users."

Norway's NRK TV channel shows include an 8-hour train ride, a 12-hour knitting show, a 12-hour log fire and 18-hours of salmon spawning.

The "proof" for 1+1=2 is 372 pages long and was not proven until the 20th century.

A 17 year old boy died in Mexico City after his girlfriend gave him a 'Hickey'

Ben Johnson the Olympic sprinter was robbed of $4900 by a gang of Gypsy children. He chased the kids, but was unable to catch them.

One of Russia's most popular '90s TV shows challenged contestants to steal a car. If they could evade police for 35 minutes, they got to keep it. The show was pulled after being linked to a rise in car thefts.

You can make up to $50,000USD a year as a professional fart-smeller in China.

When England's first escalator was installed in 1898, smelling salts and brandy were offered to customers at the top in case they had been made faint from the ride.

Nikon was accused of racist face-detection software – when Asian faces were photographed, a message would pop up on the camera screen asking, "Did someone blink?"

Squirrels masturbate to avoid catching sexually transmitted infections.

The average amount of time a woman can keep a secret is 47 hours and 15 minutes.

President Lyndon Baines Johnson named his pen*s "Jumbo", and would often show it to his staff.

Actor Nicolas Cage claims he once woke up in the middle of the night to find a naked man eating a Fudgesicle in front of his bed.

There is a bridge in Scotland where dogs are known to commit suicide. In the past fifty years, over fifty dogs have visited the bridge and leapt to their death. No one knows why.

Pineapples were such a status symbol in 18th century England that you could rent one for the evening to take to a party.

The town of Shitterton, England, changed its town sign to a 1.5 ton boulder to stop people from repeatedly stealing it.

Russia banned the sale of vodka during World War I. The government immediately lost a third of its income.

After being deposed by the Soviet Union in 1940, the President of Estonia was sent to a psychiatric hospital in Russia for "persistent claiming of being the President of Estonia".

The Scottish parliament and the Tourist Board of Scotland in 2007 spent £125,000 coming up with the slogan "Welcome to Scotland"

Zookeepers in Spain installed a TV set in their chimp Gina's cage and then taught her to use a remote. While channel surfing, Gina discovered the porn station, to which she is now addicted.

When McDonald's set up its first restaurants in Soviet Russia, it had to teach workers how to smile and pretend to be cheerful.

Russia trained dolphins to kill people with harpoons and then sold them to Iran after running out of dolphin food.

Kim Jong-un's older brother lost his favour to succeed because he was caught attempting to use a fake passport to go to Japan's Tokyo Disneyland.

One of North Korea's largest exports is giant statues of foreign dictators.

China has banned reincarnation without permission from the government.

In 1923, Germany's hyperinflation was so high, the exchange rate went from 9 marks to 4.2M marks to $1 USD. One German worker, who used a wheelbarrow to cart off billions of marks that were his week's wages, was robbed by thieves who stole the wheelbarrow but left the piles of cash on the curb.

Jerningham Wakefield, a New Zealand politician who was such a notorious drunk, his friends would lock him in Parliament overnight to keep him sober enough to vote the next day. However, this failed in 1872 when his political enemies began lowering bottles of whisky down the chimney.

Jazz legend George Melly once asked Mick Jagger why his face was so wrinkled. Jagger told him they were "laughter lines". Melly replied "Nothing's that funny."

The singer Drake's nickname among his fans in China is "gōng yā", literally "male duck", while Kanye West's nickname in China is "kǎn yé", which in Beijing dialect means "someone who brags a lot with no actions to follow it up".

The average man will spend nearly a year of his life simply staring at women.

A man stayed drunk during the entire Civil War to avoid being drafted.

The CIA operation to invade Cuba and take down Castro was dubbed "Operation Castration."

A University of Montreal study on the p*rn-viewing habits of men was cancelled when the researcher was unable to find any men who had never watched p*rn.

In 1981 Turkish scientists concluded that disco music made mice homosexual.

Members of the Mafia are much less likely to be psychopaths than other Italian criminals.

In Ancient Greece, small pen*ses were desirable, and big ones were for "old men and barbarians".

British spies used semen as invisible ink during WWI. The method was invented by Captain Sir Mansfield Cumming.

Thirty-six armed dolphins trained by the U.S. Navy to kill terrorists have been missing since 2005. The dolphins carry "toxic dart guns" capable of killing a man in a single shot.

Pimps wear lots of gold jewelry bought at pawn shops to "re-pawn" for bail money since cash is confiscated upon arrest but jewelry is not.

Former US President Calvin Coolidge enjoyed "buzzing for his bodyguards and then hiding under his desk as they frantically searched for him."

The first president of Zimbabwe was named President Banana.

A company in England accidentally sent letters to some of its wealthy customers that began "Dear Rich Bastard". One customer who did not receive the letter complained, certain their wealth was enough to warrant the "rich bastard" title.

Japan requires citizens between the ages of 45 and 74 to have their waistlines measured once a year and are expected to fall within an established range. Companies and local governments may face fines if their employees are overweight and do not meet these guidelines.

The last duel in Canada was between two men who were so terrified of dueling, one fainted and the other was seized by horror. The guns were also loaded with blanks.

In 1996, a man broke into a radio station in New Zealand, held the manager hostage, and demanded the station to play "Rainbow Connection" by Kermit the frog.

In 18th century England, the wealthy hired "ornamental hermits" to wander their land and act eccentric for guests' amusement.

A woman in Scotland registered herself by accident as a tourist attraction, becoming the nations 87th best destination.

The average Bugatti customer has about 84 cars, 3 jets and one yacht.

Paul von Lettow-Vorbeck, the respected commander of German forces in East Africa during WW1 was offered a job by Hitler in 1935. He told Hitler to "go f*ck himself" though other reports say he didn't "put it that politely."

A Florida man tossed an alligator through a drive-thru window. He was charged with "assault with a deadly weapon."

Jerry Seinfeld offered to voice a character on South Park, but later declined after Matt Stone and Trey Parker had only offered him the part of "turkey #2"

Whipping Tom was the name given to two serial spankers in London in the 17th & 18th centuries. "On seeing an unaccompanied woman, he would grab her, lift her dress, and slap her buttocks repeatedly before fleeing. He would sometimes accompany his attacks by shouting "Spanko!""

Because the number 8 is considered very lucky in Chinese culture, a Chinese man spent the equivalent of $145,000 to secure a license plate reading '88888' in the hope of increasing his luck. On his first day with the plate, he was pulled over 8 times by cops who thought the plate was a fake.

There's a version of "The Tortoise and the Hare" where everyone dies in a forest fire because the tortoise, having won the race and therefore seen as the fastest, is given the job of warning everyone.

Marlon Brando was in an acting class that was told to act like chickens and that a nuclear bomb was about to fall on them. Most of the class clucked wildly, but Brando sat calmly and pretended to lay an egg. When Stella Adler asked why he said, "I'm a chicken, What do I know about bombs?"

In 1950, residents in Mosinee, Wisconsin held a mock Communist invasion which had concentration camps, a purged library, and inflated prices. The mayor, seemingly unaware of the plan, died due to the excitement.

After Kanye interrupted Taylor Swift, Comedy Central replayed the episode "Fishsticks" four times consecutively.

In Japan, unmarried women in their late 20's were called "Christmas Cakes" because "after the 25th they're not good".

Most Japanese schools do not employ janitors or custodians. The Japanese education system believes that requiring students to clean the school themselves teaches respect, responsibility, and emphasizes equality.

Jonathan Lee Riches, a prisoner, has filed more than 4,000 lawsuits. After hearing the Guinness World Records planned to name him the "most litigious man," he sued them too.

Winston Churchill's last words were "I'm so bored with it all."

Instead of "Once upon a time," many Korean folktales begin with "Back when tigers used to smoke…"

A man named Robert Lane named his two sons "Winner" and "Loser." Winner grew up to be a criminal, and Loser became a detective.

It is estimated that 1% of society are psychopaths.

Since 2011, there have been at least 4 incidents of people cooking meth inside of a Walmart.

A zoo in Japan once spent four years trying to mate a pair of hyenas before realizing they were both males.

There are between 25 to 50 serial killers active in the United States at any one time.

Humans are born with only two innate fears: the fear of falling and the fear of loud sounds. Every other fear is learned.

Eskimos have refrigerators. They use them to keep their food warm.

From Dr. No to Quantum of Solace, James Bond has killed 352 people and slept with 52 women.

Mozart sold more CDs in 2016 than Beyonce did.

Like people, birds that live in the city are louder, meaner, and more stressed out than their country cousins.

Small animals such as flies and hummingbirds experience time in slow motion, which is why they can avoid your newspaper swats.

The female market squid sometimes display fake testicles to avoid the advances of males.

There are 1,311 people who live in Verkhoyansk, Russia, a town with an average temperature of -45C (-50F) in January. In 2012, the town was attacked by a pack of 400 wolves.

In Finland, speeding tickets are calculated on a percentage of a person's income. This causes some Finnish millionaires to face fines of over $100,000.

Two tablespoons of honey would be enough to fuel a bee's entire flight around the world.

There are more skin cancer cases attributed to tanning beds than lung cancer cases attributed to smoking.

A Chinese general with 100 troops had to defend a town against 150,000. He told his men to hide, flung open the gates and sat on the walls playing a lute. The opposing general, certain it was a trap, ordered a retreat.

No more than 40 people live 800 feet (243 m) above the ground of New York City. It's an exclusive privilege for the super rich.

A sailor who wishes to grow a beard in the Royal Navy has to submit a 'permission to stop shaving' form. He is then allowed two weeks to 'grow a full set' before he presents himself to the Master at Arms who will decide if his beard looks stupid or is respectably full enough to be permitted.

A guy made a chicken sandwich literally from scratch — he grew a garden, harvested wheat, slaughtered a chicken, travelled to boil

ocean water for salt, etc — it took him 6 months and cost him
$1,500. He didn't think it tasted very good.

In 2014, Taylor Swift accidentally released 8 seconds of white noise
on iTunes for $1.29. It became #1 in Canada almost immediately
before being removed.

The "Golden Age Fallacy" (believing the past is better than the
present) has been a popular myth that goes back as far as Ancient
Greece and Prehistoric Times.

A man, after surviving 33 days lost at sea, finally came ashore by
chance on the Marshall Islands only to discover that his uncle,
believed lost at sea 50 years ago, had washed ashore on the same
island and started a family there.

Starbucks has a different logo for Saudi Arabia because the original logo shows "too much female flesh".

Portions of Anne Frank's diary were removed because she described her intimate parts.

After reviewing all episodes of TV Show "Friends", it has been estimated Joey owed Chandler about US$114,260.

In medieval Germany, married couples could legally settle their disputes by fighting a Marital Duel. To even the field, the man had to fight from inside a hole with one arm tied behind his back. The woman was free to move and was armed with a sack filled with rocks.

Some restaurants in China lace their food with opiates to keep customers coming back.

The Dance Fever of 1518 was a month-long plague of inexplicable dancing in Strasbourg, in which hundreds of people danced for about a month for no apparent reason. Several of them danced themselves to death.

It is a criminal offence to drive around in a dirty car in Russia.

During the American Civil War, visiting prostitutes was called enjoying "horizontal refreshments."

"Sutton's Law" states "that when diagnosing, one should consider the obvious". Named after the famous American bank robber, Willie Sutton, when asked 'Why do you rob banks?' To which he replied, 'Because that's where the money is.'

Slovakia and Slovenia are mistakenly thought to be each other so often they meet once a month to exchange wrongly addressed mail.

In 1994, a 75-pound bag of cocaine fell out of a plane and landed in the middle of a Florida crime watch meeting.

In Texas, it is legal to kill BigFoot if you ever find it.

A San Diego park's monorail was named the Wgasa Rail Line after managers requested an African-sounding name. WGASA is an acronym for "Who gives a sh*t anyways?"

Under Delaware state law a marriage can be annulled if either partner entered into the marriage as a dare.

33% of US Tourists visiting Scotland believe the Haggis is an actual animal, and a quarter thought they could catch one.

19th century England had 'Ugly Clubs' where people that had less desirable facial traits met up to drink, sing, and satirize their own looks.

In Japan, you can hire handsome men to show up at your office and watch sad videos with you until you cry, then wipe your tears for you.

Because of a lucky genetic mutation that happened in the 18th century, today 38 people in a small town in northern Italy don't suffer from cholesterol artery-clogging, making them virtually immune to heart disease and strokes. They all smoke, they eat like hell, and they don't care.

In 2013, Al-Qaeda apologised for accidentally beheading one of their own men.

In 2006, a man in Sudan was ordered to marry a goat after he was caught having sex with it.

In order to discover that penguins sleep more deeply in the afternoon, scientists crept up on sleeping penguins at different times of the day and poked them with a stick until they woke up.

Adding salt to a pineapple will actually cause it to taste sweeter. It reduces the bitterness of the fruit.

Nearly 1 in 10 Americans has severe anger issues and access to guns.

The Finnish word 'pilkunnussija', literally translated as "comma f*cker", is a person who corrects grammar at the peril of their own social standing.

The Korean version of "LOL" is "KKK".

A Taliban leader once listed "jihad" as a skill on the social network LinkedIn.

A Canadian band sent a bill to the U.S. Government requesting US$666,000 in royalties for playing their music as torture for Guantanamo Bay's prisoners.

A Polish man lived with a bullet in his head for 5 years after forgetting he was shot at a party.

In 2013, a burglar in Oklahoma used the toilet and forgot to flush. He was caught after being identified by DNA.

7% of all American adults believe that chocolate milk comes from brown cows, a survey found.

Housing a prisoner in California costs $75,560. That's more than a year at Harvard.

John Adams, 2nd president of the USA, started smoking at the age of eight.

Cockroaches appeared 120 million years before dinosaurs.

You're 1,000 times more likely to be killed by an asteroid than to win the lottery.

Speed dating was invented by a Rabbi in 1999.

The motto on the very first official United States coin was "Mind Your Business".

In the Chinese city of Chongqing, Smartphone addicts have their own sidewalk lane.

Heartbreak is actually a form of addiction withdrawal.

Farmers in Botswana have started painting eyes on their cows bottoms to stop lions from attacking them.

After a duelling, it's common for two male giraffes to have sex with each other. Such interactions between males have been found to be more frequent than heterosexual coupling,

Female-named hurricanes kill more than male-named hurricanes because people don't respect them, a study found.

In Mississippi it's illegal to have more than one child out of wedlock.

In Russia, Jews were believed to have a secret vegetable they eat so they don't become alcoholics. Anti-semitism was justified because they refused to share their "magic vegetable."

The word 'censorship' is censored in China.

Barbara is Latin for "strange woman."

The combined wealth of the 85 richest people is equal to that of poorest 3.5 billion --half of the world's population.

Sending a man to the Moon and finding Osama Bin Laden cost the US government about the same amount of time and money: 10 years and $100 billion.

Originally, the wedding cake was not eaten, but thrown at the bride.

Hours before being assassinated on April 4, 1968, Martin Luther King Jr. took part in a motel pillow fight.

Spiny lobsters migrate in large groups forming conga-like lines on the sea floor.

Male millipedes court females with songs and back rubs.

Superman was originally a bald villain.

Mike Tyson became a boxer because a bully killed his pigeon.

You can find the sources for all the facts in this paperback book in the Kindle version of this book. When you buy the paperback version you are entitled to a free Kindle version of this book. You can access the Kindle version of this book from the Amazon account you used to buy this paperback book.

If you enjoyed this book or received value from it in any way, then I'd like to ask you for a favor: would you be kind enough to leave a review for this book on Amazon? It'd be greatly appreciated!

25787320R00039

Printed in Great Britain
by Amazon